THOUGHTS OF MY SOUL ON A PAPER OF GOLD

SEHAJ KAUR

Copyright © Sehaj Kaur
All Rights Reserved.

ISBN 979-888606266-3

It was raining hail

you were returning home

from your grave

you watched as your life slipped away

like a bottle of vine

red splattered everywhere

the truth was always right in front

you just had to look in the right direction

and I remember everything

the way the glass broke

the way it shattered

the intensity of the sound

the crumbles that were left on the floor

no one even noticed

no one really cared

you were always enough

a warrior

a survivor

I will always remember you.

THIS BOOK IS DEDICATED TO MY YOUNGER SELF

THE GIRL I WILL ALWAYS REMEMBER AND LOVE DEARLY

THIS IS FOR YOU

YOU WERE ALWAYS ENOUGH FOR ME.

Contents

Contents

Contents

Preface

I STARTED TO WRITE POETRY,

AS A WAY TO EXPRESS WHAT I WAS FEELING

I UNDERSTOOD MYSELF BETTER BY THIS.

AS I STARTED WRITING

I DISCOVERED THAT,

WRITING DOWN WHATEVER CAME TO MY MIND

HELPED ME DEAL WITH COMPL;EX EMOTIONS

AND

PROBLEMS THAT I BURIED DEEP WITHIN MY CONSCIOUS.

THESE POETRY'S ARE MERELY MY THOUGHTS ON A PAPER,

THAT IS HOW I CAME UP WITH THE TITLE ~

THOUGHTS OF MY SOUL ON A PAPER OF GOLD.

THIS BOOK DEALS WITH ISSUES LIKE

    SELF - HATE

    BULLYING

    EMOTIONAL TRAUMA

I HOPE YOU LIKE IT

THANKS FOR READING

~ SEHAJ KAUR.

Acknowledgements

SO THIS IS FOR THE ONES WHO MATTER ALOT TO ME IN LIFE.

FIRSTLY TO

MY BEST FRIEND,

THANK YOU SO MUCH FOR JUST BEING THERE FIRST OF ALL,

BECAUSE YOU WERE THE ONE WHO INSPIRED ME TO ACTUALLY WRITE THIS BOOK.

YOU WERE THE ONE WHO ENCOURAGED ME,

ALWAYS BELIEVED IN ME,

MOTIVATED ME THROUGHOUT.

SO HERE I AM,

ALL THANKS TO YOU.

I AM GRATEFUL FOR EVERYTHING,

AND

I AM BLESSED TO HAVE A FRIEND LIKE YOU IN MY LIFE.

HERE'S TO

MY BROTHER,

SO THIS ONE WAS REALLY HARD TO PUT INTO WORDS

BUT HERE IT IS,

SO THANKS FOR BEING THE BEST BROTHER IN THE WHOLE WORLD.

BEING THE ONE WHO I COULD ALWAYS BLINDLY TRUST.

AND I WILL ALWAYS BE GRATEFUL FOR EVERY PART OF ADVICE YOU GAVE ME

WHILE I WAS WRITING THIS BOOK,

EVERY BIT OF ENCOURAGMENT

AND FAITH YOU SHOWED IN ME.

YOU WERE THE ONLY ONE WHO READ THIS BOOK BEFORE IT GOT PUBLISHED,

AND THE FIRST ONE TO KNOW ABOUT THIS PROJECT.

THANK YOU FOR HELPING ME WITH ALL THE ILLUSTRATIONS

AND SOLVING EVERY SMALL PROBLEM THAT I FACED WHILE EDITING,

AND CONTINOUSLY BICKERED ABOUT.

THANKYOU FOR BEING PATIENT WITH ME.

I AM GRATEFUL FOR YOU

AND

YOU WILL ALWAYS BE MY ROCK.

FINALLY TO

MY PARENTS,

MOM AND DAD

I LOVE YOU

I AM GRATEFUL FOR YOU,

AND EVERYTHING YOU DO FOR ME.

I AM BLESSED TO HAVE SUCH SUPPORTING PARENTS

THANK YOU FOR BEING THE WAY YOU ARE

I COULDN'T HAVE ASKED FOR ANYTHING ELSE.

1. ~ ~ ~ ~ IT BEGINS WITH A HIT TO THE GUT ~ ~ ~ ~

THIS CHAPTER IS ABOUT HOW I STARTED TO BOTTLE UP MY EMOTIONS, HOW IT ALL STARTED TO TAKE A TOLL ON MY MENTAL HEALTH AND HOW I STARTED TO BELIEVE THE PEOPLE WHO WANTED NOTHING MORE TO BRING ME DOWN AND GUESS WHAT?
THEY SUCCEEDED

2. FLAMES

HANG YOUR HEAD LOW
THEY WON'T NOTICE
SCREAMED FOR WHATEVER IT'S WORTH,
NO ONE HEARD
KEPT MY EMOTIONS AT BAY
SECRETS KEPT DEEP WITHIN ME,
I AM NOT DYING.

3. TREPIDATION

I TRY EVERYDAY
SHIVERS DOWN MY SPINE,
THIS HAUNTING FEAR SWALLOWING ME WHOLE,
LEFT ALONE
IN MY OWN HOME.

4. BLACK & WHITE

THE PICTURE IS QUITE CLEAR
DULL MEMORIES HANG IN THE BACKGROUND
BLACK FACES HAUNTING ME AS IT GOES,
SHRILL VOICES SCREAMING AT ME FOR HELP,
THE GLASS BREAKS FROM ALL THE NOICE,
THE LIGHT COMING FROM THE WINDOW,
NOW SCATTERED ACROSS THE ROOM.
FORCED TO GET AWAY TO DANCE IN THE MOONLIGHT
WHITE SPOTS INVADE MY VISION,
AS I REACH HIGHER UP IN THE SKY
BREATHING BECOMES MORE PAIN-FREE

&

AS I LOOKED BACK UPON THE WORLD,
I SEE THEM RUNNING FOR THEIR LIVES
I SAW THE MADNESS UNFOLD AS IT FINALLY CAME TO AN
END
LOOKING AT IT, IN THIS MOMENT OF TRUTH
IT'S A BEAUTIFULL GOODBYE

5. CHANGES

I STARTED EXPECTING AGAIN
DISAPPOINTMENT WAS BOUND TO HAPPEN SOMEDAY,
THOUGHT IT WAS ALL IN THE PAST
I CHANGED.
I DON'T KNOW WHAT TO DO TO BE ACCEPTED,
WHAT AM I SUPPOSED TO BE?

6. PREY

IN A ROOM FULL OF PEOPLE
STILL ALONE
THIS PIT IN MY STOMACH ONLY GROWS.
HEAVY BREATHS,
SHAKY HANDS,
THEY CONTINUE ALL THE BULLYING
TEARING ME APART WITH EVERY WORD THEY SAY.
I TRY BUT, NEVER GET FAR
I SHOULD HAVE KNOWN,
I WOULD BE THE FIRST ONE TO LEAVE.
THE GREAT PRISON BREAK,
FLYING HIGH TO GET AWAY,
I AM THE ONLY PREY IN THIS HUNT.

7. ~ ~ ~ ~ THROUGH THE DARK PASSAGE ~ ~ ~ ~

THIS CHAPTER IS ALL ABOUT GIVING UP.
WHEN THE DARK COVERS THE LIGHT,
WHEN THE WATER IS TOO FAR UP YOUR HEAD AND YOU
ARE DROWNING IN YOUR OWN GUILTS.
WHEN YOU START BELIEVING THAT YOU WILL NEVER BE
ENOUGH.
WHEN YOU LOSE HOPE.

8. ANTIDOTE

SEAS OF EYES
FOCUSED ON MY CRIES
I FLY INTO THE THE SKIES,
CAUSE I DON'T WANNA BE ALONE
I CAN FEEL THEM TAKING CONTROL
LOVING IS THE ANTIDOTE
HURTS BUT IT'S OKAY
I'll GET MY WAY ONE DAY.

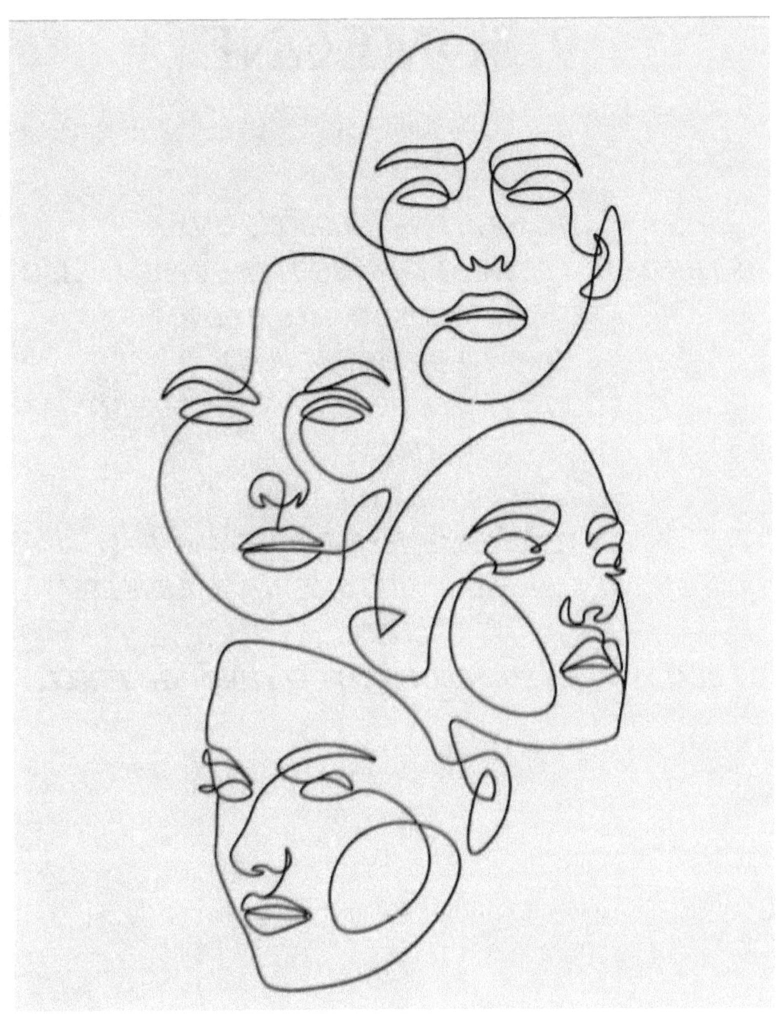

9. SOMEONE

*THIS NIGHT NEVER GROWS OLD
AS THE DAY BLEEDS AND THIS NIGHT UNFOLDS, I REALLY
NEED SOMEBODY TO CALL MY OWN,
JUST TO SEE HOW IT FEELS.
AND THIS CONSTRICTED FEELING IN MY CHEST ONLY
GROWS
I WANNA FADE AWAY,
JUST TO BE REMEMBERED BY SOMEONE.
WHEN THE SUN STARTS SETTING AND THE SKY FEELS
COLD,*
I REALLY NEED SOMEBODY TO GO THROUGH IT ALL.

10. SLOW POISION

THEY WOULD ALWAYS HAVE REASONS TO
BELIEVE THAT I WAS WRONG.
POINTING FINGERS AT ME,
THEY WON'T UNDERSTAND MY MISERY.
SLOW POISON FROM THE ONES I HOLD DEARLY.

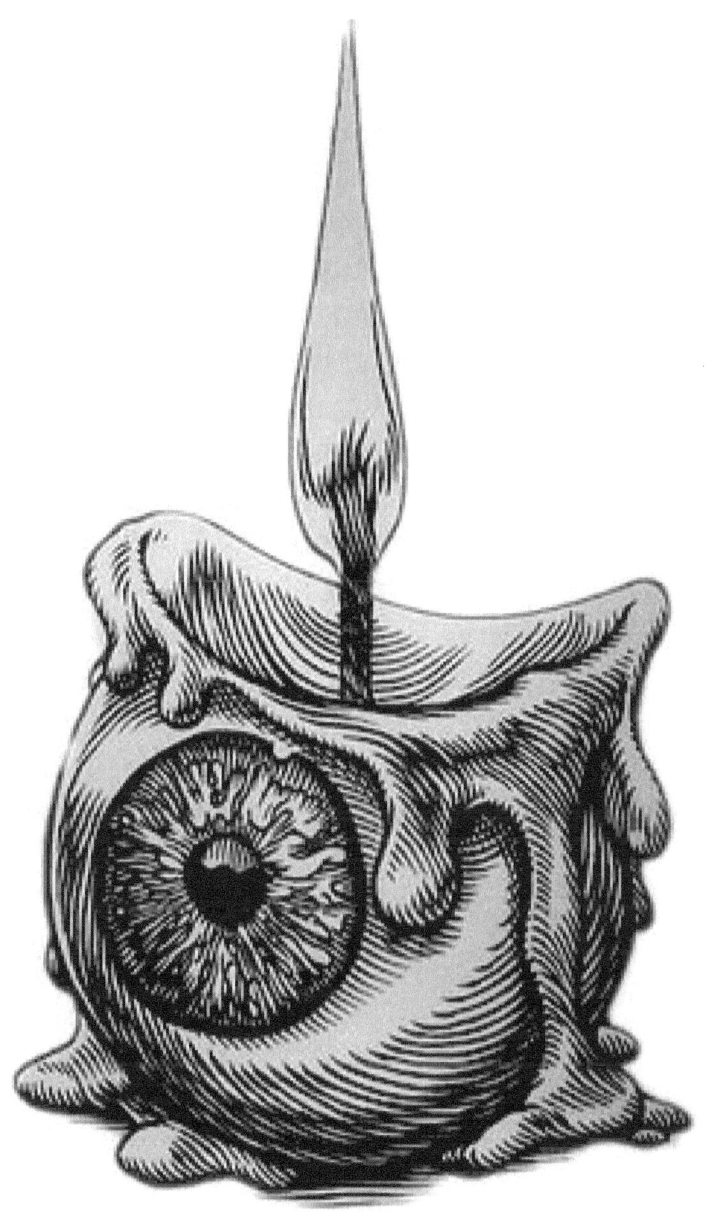

11. COLLAPSE

*I FEEL THE DARK WATERS TAKING CONTROL
BREATHING IN MY OWN BODY MAKES MY SKIN CRAWL,
I SINK DEEPER INTO THIS PROFOUND FEELING OF NOT
BEING ENOUGH.
THE WEIGHT ON MY BACK IS MAKING ME DROWN INTO
THE SHADOWS,
IT IS NOT SOMETHING I IMAGINED MYSELF GOING
THROUGH
I WANT TO GIVE UP, LET GO
BE FREE FROM ALL THE CHAOS IN MY LIFE.
BUT SOMETHING KEPT ME GOING
SOMETHING IN ME WANTED TO TRY ONE LAST TIME
BEFORE,*
GIVING UP THE LAST SHRED OF HOPE LEFT WITHIN ME.

12. ~ ~ ~ ~ SELF-NEGLECT

~ ~ ~ ~

THIS CHAPTER IS ALL ABOUT NOT BEING ABLE TO ACCEPT YOURSELF.
NOT APPRECIATING WHAT YOU DID OR SUCEEDED TO DO AND JUST FOCUSING ON WHAT YOU COULDN'T DO.
CREATING UNREALISTIC EXPECTATIONS FROM YOURSELF.
ALWAYS HAVING THIS EMPTY FEELING OR JUST THIS PIT IN YOUR STOMACH,
JUST THIS CONSTANT ANXIETY OF NOT DOING ENOUGH.
HOW DO YOU EXPECT OTHER'S TO LOVE AND ACCEPT YOU,
WHEN YOU CAN'T EVEN LOVE OR ACCEPT YOURSELF.

13. FLOWERS

FLOWERS SO BEAUTIFUL,
SO COLOURFUL, SO SOULFUL.
ONE DAY I WAS WONDERING
CAN I HAVE THEM ALL?
THE MERE THOUGHT RUINED IT ALL
OH! ALL THE FLOWERS JUST DIED,
THEY ARE NOW RESERVED JUST AS A SWEET MEMORY,
DEATH BEDS COVERED BY THEM.
FLOWERS SO DULL,
SO OLD, SO SHRIVELLED.
I WONDERED IF I STAYED HAPPY
WITH WHAT I HAD AND
DIDN'T ASK FOR IT ALL.

14. SELF-SABOTAGE

SACRIFICING MY OWN HAPPINESS,
TO BE MATTERED FOR ONCE.
MY STORY STARTS WITH A GIRL WHO ONCE BELIEVED IN
HERSELF,
NOW IT'S STUCK ON SOME SELF LOATHING, SOCIAL
SUICIDE THAT CAN'T HELP BUT FEEL LONELY ALL THE
TIME.
BUT SHE IS AN ACTRESS SO SHE PRETENDS,
TILL SHE FORGETS WHO SHE WAS.
I LOOK IN THE MIRROR AND I AM SO OVER IT,
EVERY RIGHT STEP I TAKE GOES TO WASTE
AS I AM A SELF-SABOTAGING EMOTIONAL WRECK.
THIS STORY ENDS WITH ME TRYING TO SAVE ME FROM
MYSELF.

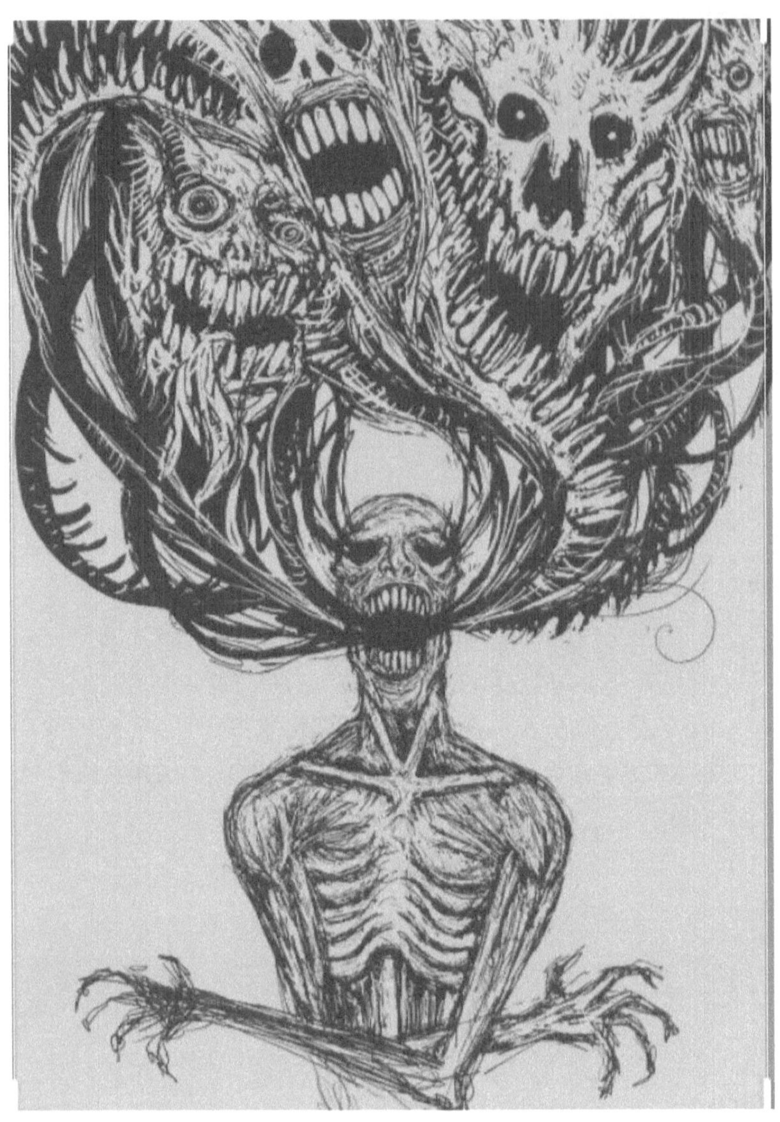

15. ADDICTIVE

SELF HATING IS ADDICTIVE
IT STARTED AS MINOR CRITICISM
NEVER KNEW IT COULD BE SO DANGEROUS.
IT'S BEEN A WHILE SINCE I LOOKED IN THE MIRROR
CREATING A PLACE IN MY HEAD WHERE I FEEL GOOD, MY
SAFE HAVEN.
I THINK I AM ALLERGIC TO MYSELF
NEVER KNEW SKIN TIGHT DRESSES WOULD BE SUCH A
PAINFUL SIGHT TO BEAR.
I THINK I COULD MOVE ON FROM THIS HELL LOOP IF I
TRIED,
BUT I DON'T KNOW HOW TO.
YOU KNOW HOW THERE IS ALWAYS A VILLAIN IN A STORY,
WELL I AM THE VILLAIN IN MINE.

16. MEMORY LANE

I WALK DOWN THIS MEMORY LANE
TO REMEMBER HOW I WAS
FULL OF LIFE,
FULL OF LOVE,
NOTHING FEARED ME
NOTHING FELT ROT.
WHISPERS OF PEOPLE THAT I FORGOT ABOUT,
I AM SUCH A SOCIAL SUICIDE.
THE PERFECT IMAGE IS TOO HARD TO ACHIEVE
THESE SCARS ARE TOO DEEP TO HIDE.
SO I WALK DOWN MEMORY LANE
TO REMEMBER WHAT IT WAS LIKE AGAIN.

17. MY LOVE

*TO FEEL SOMETHING IS SO MUCH BETTER TO NOT FEEL
ANYTHING AT ALL
BOUNDLESS BY THE TIME I CRIED,
BUILT MY WALLS AROUND ME.
COULD I FEEL SOMETHING
I KNOW NOTHING OF AT ALL?
CURSED BY THE LOVE THAT I RECEIVE
ALL THESE MEMORIES OF MY LOVE CLOUD ME
NOW I AM PRONE TO ALL THE MISERY.
NOW THE RIVER BED HAS DRIED
LOOKING EVERYWHERE IN SEARCH OF WATER,
IT REMINDS ME OF US
LOOKING FOR SOMETHING THEY HAD ALL ALONG.
HOW MUCH SORROW CAN I TAKE?
AND WHAT DIFFERENCE DOES IT MAKE,
WHEN I HAVE TO DIE ONE DAY ALL ALONG.
THE LAST BREATH I TAKE,
WOULD BE TO REMEMBER ALL THE MEMORIES OF*
MY LOVE.

18. ~ ~ ~ ~ PATH TO REALIZATION ~ ~ ~ ~

*THIS CHAPTER FOCUSES ON HOW YOU START TO REALISE
WHAT YOU ARE DOING WRONG,
BUT YOU STILL AREN'T READY TO ACCEPT IT.
IT'S WHEN YOU REALISE THAT YOU ARE HUMAN AND YOU
CAN ASK FOR HELP.*
***ASKING FOR HELP DOESN'T SHOW THAT YOU ARE WEAK,
IT SHOWS THAT YOU ARE STRONG ENOUGH TO ACCEPT
YOUR VULNERABLE SIDE.***

19. JUST A LITTLE KID

I AM JUST A LITTLE KID,
I AM NOT UP FOR IT ALL.
THIS WORLD IS JUST A BIG MAGIC TRICK,
WE ARE JUST THE PUPPETS AND SOMEONE UP THERE IS
PULLING OUR STRINGS.
WHEN I FEEL LONELY,
I WANT TO BE ALONE
CAUSE THERE'S ONLY ME
WHO I CAN CALL MY OWN.
I AM NOT READY FOR THE STRUGGLES OF LIFE,
I JUST WANT TO HOLD ONTO THIS KID FOR A LITTLE
WHILE MORE.

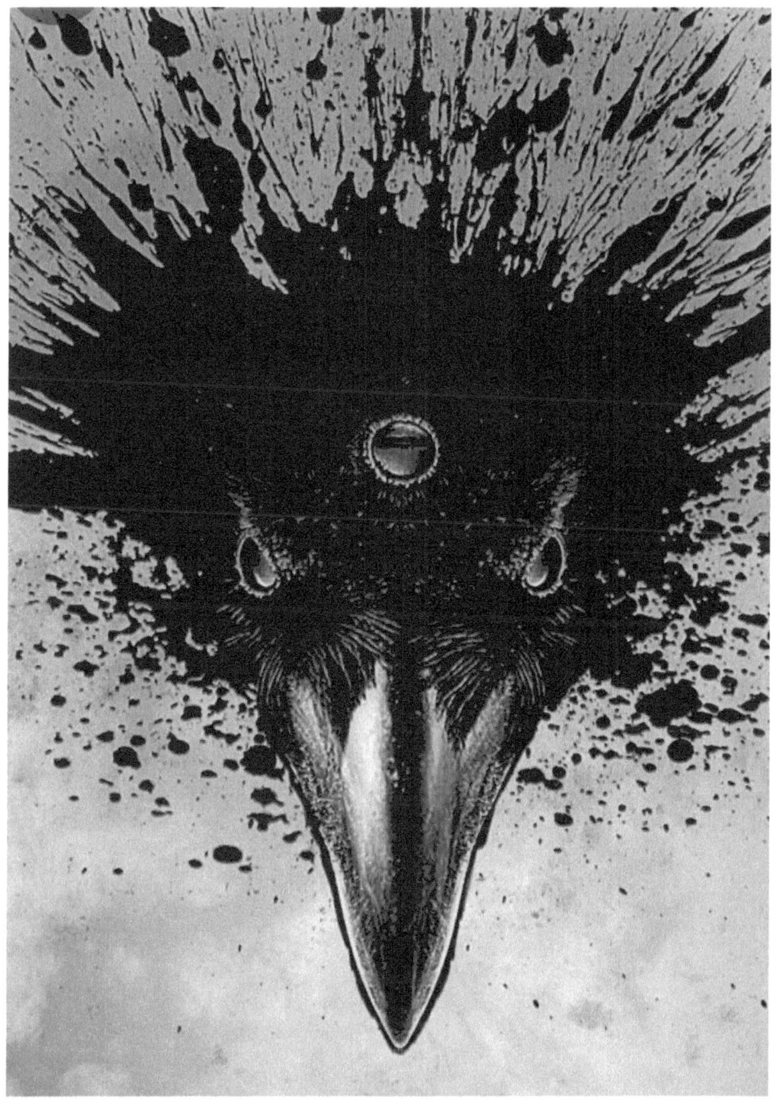

20. END OF THE YEAR

IT'S THE END OF THE YEAR,
AND I FEEL LIKE I AM NOTHING AGAINST MY PEERS.
USUALLY I DON'T ASK FOR HELP
BUT THIS CHARADE OF NOT NEEDING ANYONE,
IS CRUMBLING DOWN WITH EVERY TEAR.
I THOUGHT LIFE WAS SUPPOSED TO BE FUN
BUT ALL I WANNA DO IS RUN.

21. LIES

SHE'S SO FUN TO BE AROUND
SHE ALWAYS GETS ALONG WITH EVERYONE,
SHE TALKS FOR HOURS WHEN NOBODY IS EVEN
LISTENING.
BUT QUITE WHEN SHE'S COMING HOME
WHEN SHE'S ALL ALONE.
I COULD LIE AND SAY THAT I LIKE IT LIKE THAT.
THIS BLEEDING NEVER STOPS,
HEALING NEVER STARTS.
I COULD LIE AND SAY THAT I LIKE IT LIKE THAT.
CALL ME A FRIEND BUT TREAT ME LIKE A STRANGER.
TELL ME YOUR PROBLEMS, YOU KNOW I WOULD SOLVE
THEM
I SHOULD'VE KNOWN BETTER TO ASK FOR THE SAME
THING IN RETURN.
I COULD LIE AND SAY THAT I LIKE IT LIKE THAT.

22. FEELINGS

SUBTLE FEELINGS
ON THE ROAD TO HEALING
CAN'T PROCESS WHAT I AM FEELING
I DON'T DO ENOUGH
WHAT I DO TIRES ME
I SEELP FOR HOURS
THE TIME WON'T STOP FOR ME
THIS PRESSURE ONLY BUILDS,
AS THE DAY TURNS TO DAWN.

23. I WONDER

DREAMING A WORLD FULL OF LIFE.
I WONDER WHAT IT'S LIKE,
A WORLD THAT'S NOT BLACK AND WHITE
PEACEFUL LIVES, CALM MINDS
REALITY THAT ISN'T CATASTROPHIC
POWER THAT'S GOOD,
SIMPLE THAT'S NOT DULL,
EQUALITY THAT'S NOT HYPOCRITE,
STRONG THAT'S NOT EVIL,
CLARITY THAT DOESN'T CAUSE ME TO RUN FOR MY LIFE,
LOVE THAT'S UNCONDITIONAL.
I WONDER IF I WOULD BE ABLE TO LIVE LIFE.

24. ~ ~ ~ ~ PATH TO RESTORATION ~ ~ ~ ~

THIS CHAPTER IS ABOUT WHEN YOU START WORKING ON YOURSELF RATHER THAN JUST SITTING AND PITYING YOURSELF.

WHEN YOU START TO LOOK FORWARD IN THE FUTURE RATHER THAN BEING STUCK IN THE PAST.

WHEN YOU START BELIEVING IN LIFE ITSELF.

LIFE IS A GIFT

YOU ARE HERE FOR A REASON.

25. ALONE FEELS RIGHT

SOMETIMES,
ALONE FEEL RIGHT.
THE DOOR NOW CLOSED,
FEELS RIGHT TO BE THE ONLY ONE IN THE ROOM.
AT PEACE,
WITH THEMSELVES.
DOING WHATEVER YOU WANT,
IT'S BEAUTIFULLY SILENT.
HEART AT PEACE,
MIND AT REST.
ALONE FEELS RIGHT.

26. EVERY STAR HAS A WISH TRAPPED IN IT

I FEEL GOLDEN.
SPARKLY STARS LOOKING AT ME,
BUT THEY WERE FAR TOO BRIGHT FOT THE EYES.
SMILING I KEEP GOING
FACING THE WORLD ALONE,
I CAN FEEL THE DARKNESS TAKING CONTROL.
THE STARS SHINE BRIGHTER TONIGHT,
TRAPPING EVERY WISH I EVER MADE.
THEY ARE SO FAR AWAY,
BUT I'll TRAVEL EVERY MILE
HOPING ONE DAY I'll REACH THE LIGHT.

27. NEW YEAR

*IT'S A NEW YEAR AND THERE'S NOTHING I LOOK FORWARD
TO
CREATING THIS BARRIER, BETWEEN ME AND MY FEELINGS
TO SEEM HAPPY ON THE EXTERIOR.
I AM WIDE AWAKE AT NIGHT, THINKING ABOUT
THE NEXT DAYLIGHT.
BUT WHEN THE TIME COMES, I AM NOT READY TO FACE
WHAT'S WAITING FOR ME.
I NEED SOMETHING TO FEEL SAFE*
**SAFE IN THIS UNCERTAIN WORLD THAT IS FULL OF
WHAT IFS.**

28. ~ ~ ~ ~ BEING MY OWN DARK NIGHT ~ ~ ~ ~

THIS CHAPTER IS ABOUT HOW IT ALL STARTED TO MAKE
SENSE.
THERE WOULD ALWAYS BE BAD DAYS OF COURSE,
BUT I LEARNED THAT THEY ARE A PART OF LIFE.
A VERY IMORTANT PART MIGHT I ADD.
THESE BAD DAYS ARE A PART OF OUR GROWTH,
TO BEING OUR BEST SELVES.
IT MADE ME STRONGER AT THE END OF THE DAY.
EVERY BAD DAY WAS A LESSON IN ITSELF.
YOU ARE ART
AND ART WASN'T EVER MADE TO BE PERFECT.
IT WAS MADE TO BE REAL, FULL OF EVERY KIND OF
EMOTION.
YOU ARE ART
YOUR IMPERFECTIONS ARE SOMETHING THAT MAKE
YOU PERFECT.

29. GRACE

HEY PRETTY MISS
I SEE THE WAY YOUR EYES SPARKLE,
LIKE THE DAYLIGHT BEAM.
MOONLIT FACE WITH HAIR LIKE THE NIGHT WAVES.
AS SERENE, PEACEFUL AND CALMING RAIN FALLS DOWN
YOUR FACE
YOU WALK THROUGH THIS LANE ALONE
WITH ALL YOUR THOUGHTS GATHERED UP AT ONE
PLACE.
YOU ARE BEAUTIFUL
YOU ARE KIND
YOU ARE STRONG
BLISSFUL LIKE THE MORNING SUN,
CHEERY LIKE THE BIRDS,
SOFT LIKE THE LATE NIGHT BREEZE,
DREAMY LIKE THE STARLIGHT.
YOU SHINE LIKE NO OTHER
YOU ARE DETERMINED TO ALWAYS BE BETTER
YOU WORK HARD FOR BUILDING UP A FUTURE FOR
YOURSELF
IT'll PAY OFF ONE DAY BECAUSE,
YOU ARE YOUR OWN SHINNING GRACE.

30. SEA

*WASHING AWAY WITH WATER LIKE THE SAND THAT SLIPS
AWAY
THE SHORE IS SO CLATTERED, FULL OF CHAOS.
AS I SINK DEEPER, I WATCH HOW
THE DIFFERENT TONES OF BLUE MIX WITH THE CLEAR
WATERS OF THE DEATHLY SILENT SEA.
SOMETHING NEVER LOOKED SO CALMING BEFORE.
WHEN I LOOKED DOWN, I SAW THAT THERE WAS ENDLESS
WATER OF JUST NOTHING.
SO EMPTY
SO CLEAR
SO SIMPLE*

**IT WAS MESMERISING TO SEE SOMETHING BE SO
DESOLATE YET BE SO BEAUTIFUL.**

31. PLEASINGLY ME

AS I OPEN MY EYES
I SEE A CLEAR PICTURE,
UNDERSTANDING MYSELF AS THE TIME GOES BY.
I FEEL MY FEET ABOVE THE GROUND
SOFT TOUCHES OF LOVE TO ME
RUNNING ENDLESSLY ACROSS THE FIELDS.
I AM LEARNING THIS LESSON WITH EVERY PASSING DAY
I HAVE TO ACCEPT MYSELF TO BELIEVE THAT,
I AM PLEASINGLY ME.

32. HERO

YOU ARE RESPONSIBLE FOR YOURSELF
NO ONE'S GONNA COME AND SAVE YOU
YOU HAVE TO SAVE YOURSELF
FROM ALL THE CHAOS IN THIS WORLD
THE CONFUSION OF WHO TO BE AND WHO TO CHOOSE,
WHO TO TRUST AND WHO TO LET GO.
YOU HAVE TO LEARN HOW TO BE STRONG,
YOU ARE BRAVE,
MUCH MORE THAN YOU THINK YOU ARE.
CREATE THE WORLD YOU DREAM OF DAY AND NIGHT
BE THE HERO YOU WANT,
YOU ARE ALL YOU EVER NEED.

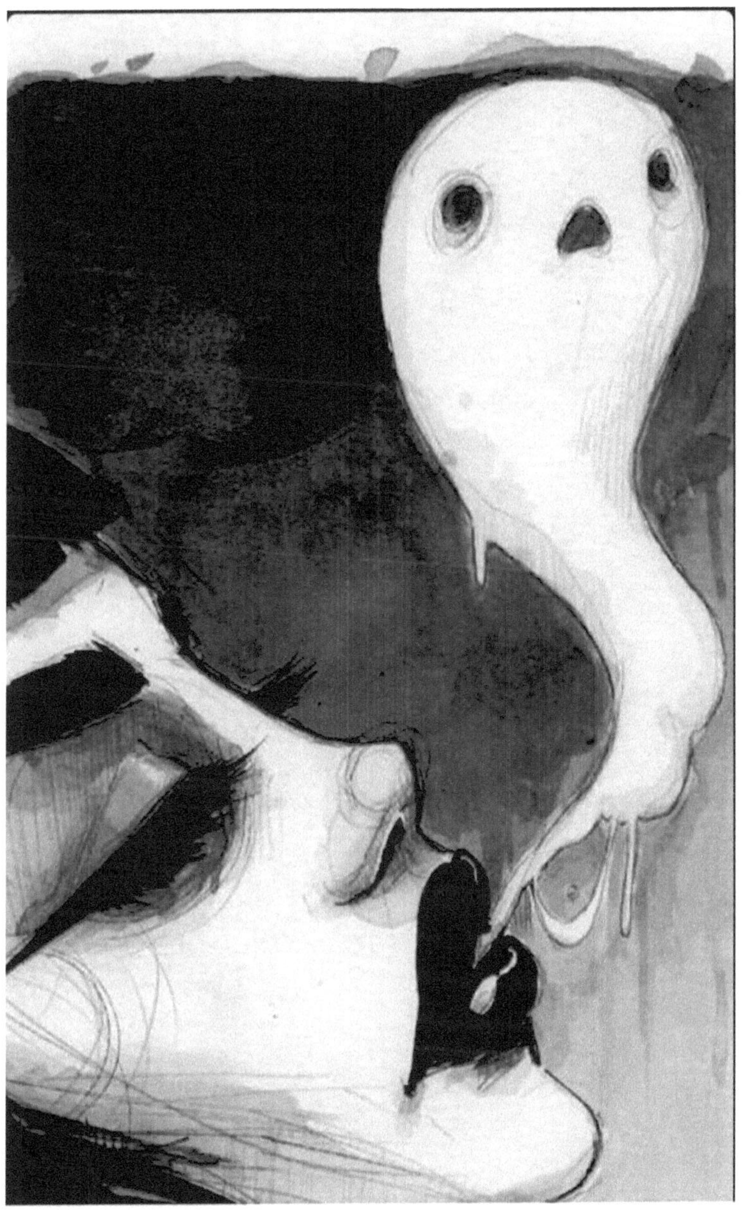

33. AFTERLIFE

AT THE END OF ALL OF THIS,
THERE IS FREEDOM.
ALL OF THIS JUST GONE
BLEAK WHITE LIGHTS IS WHAT I IMAGINE IT TO BE
SOUNDS SO CALMING
SO PEACEFUL
IT IS WHAT KEEPS ME GOING,
BEACAUSE I KNOW THAT ONE DAY THIS ALL IS GOING TO
COUNT
MISTAKES - VICTORIES - CRIMES
EVERY HEART YOU BROKE,
EVERYTHING YOU FIXED WITH LOVE.
&
WHEN THIS LIGHT REACHES YOU ONE DAY
YOU WILL BE NOTHING, JUST LIGHT THAT GUIDES
OTHERS
THAT'S WHAT I WANT TO BE ONCE I AM GONE.

34. ~ ~ ~ ~ AS I LOOK BACK UPON THE PAST ~ ~ ~ ~

*THIS CHAPTER SOLELY FOCUSES ON
HOW WHEN YOU START TO RECALL AND RECOLLECT ALL
THE MEMORIES FROM YOUR PAST.
LOOKING BACK AT YOURSELF AND REALISING
EVERYTHING THAT'S BEEN DONE.
NOW THAT YOU ARE AT A NEW STAGE IN YOUR LIFE,
AND HOW YOU HAVE TO START AGAIN FROM NOTHING.
WHEN EVERYTHING SEEMS UNRECOGNISABLE AND
UNCERTAIN.
WHEN YOU DON'T KNOW WHERE TO START FROM
BECAUSE THERE IS SO MUCH YOU WANT TO DO.
WHEN YOU DON'T KNOW WHERE YOU BELONG.*

***WHEN LIFE GIVES A YOU A NEW CHANCE
A CLEAN SLATE
BE THE PERSON YOU ALWAYS WANTED TO BE
BE THE PERSON WHO YOU WILL BE PROUD OF
YOU HAVE NOTHING TO LOSE.***

35. DEAL WITH THE DEVIL

A BROKEN PERSON WAS ALL THAT WAS LEFT,
I AM STILL FIXING UP THE CRACKS,
LOSING WHO I WAS IN THE PROCESS.
IT'S ALL CHAOS IN MY HEAD
LOST EVERY FIGHT IN THIS BATTLEFIELD
THIS RAGING WAR WITH MYSELF
SAVED WHAT I COULD SAVE
I KNEW THERE WOULD ALWAYS BE COLLATERAL DAMAGE.
I TOLD MY SELF PRETTY LIES,
TO COVER UP THE MONSTERS OF MY PAST
THOSE WHO STARE BACK AT ME
WITH MY BLOOD IN THEIR HANDS
HAUNTING ME EVERY NIGHT
I KNOW IT'S ALL FAKE;
A DECEIVING REALITY CREATED BY ME.
ALL THIS TO COPE,
WITH THE DAMAGE THAT'S ALREADY BEEN DONE.
WANTED TO BE AT PEACE WITH MYSELF,
SO I MADE A DEAL WITH THE DEVIL HIMSELF.

36. WHERE YOU BELONG

CLOSE YOUR EYES,
FEEL THE WATER AROUND YOU
YOU SEE A REFLECTION IN THE WATER,
IT'S YOU.
PAINTING A PICTURE WITH YOUR TEARS;
YOU CALL IT YOUR OWN.
WHERE DO YOU WANT TO GO,
YOU HAVE NO WHERE TO FALL.
SLOW WINDS PUSH YOU TOWARDS YOUR HOME,
WHERE YOU BELONG.

37. CLASHINGLY

I AM CHOOSING A DIFFERENT PATH TO WALK ON THIS
TIME
BECAUSE,
THE OTHER ONE IS FULL OF TORMENT.
AS I AM ABOUT TO TAKE A STEP ON THIS NEW ROAD
I THINK OF,
HOW I DON'T HAVE CLUE
WHERE IT WOULD TAKE ME.
I AM SCARED
IT'S ALL SO UNCERTAIN
AT LEAST WHEN I USED THE PREVIOUS ONE,
I KNEW WHAT WAS GOING TO HAPPEN
THERE WERE NO JUMP SCARES.
WHAT IF THIS PATH LEADS TO MORE MISERY,
MORE CHAOS.
ALL THIS INNER TURMOIL I GO THROUGH,
TO CHOOSE WHICH LANE TO GO ON.
ONE IS FULL OF UNCERTAINTY,
ONE IS FULL OF PAIN AND AGONY.
MY MIND AND HEART
ACT SO CLASHINGLY,
ONE WANTS TO BE HELD CAPTIVE
OTHER WANTS TO BREAK FREE.

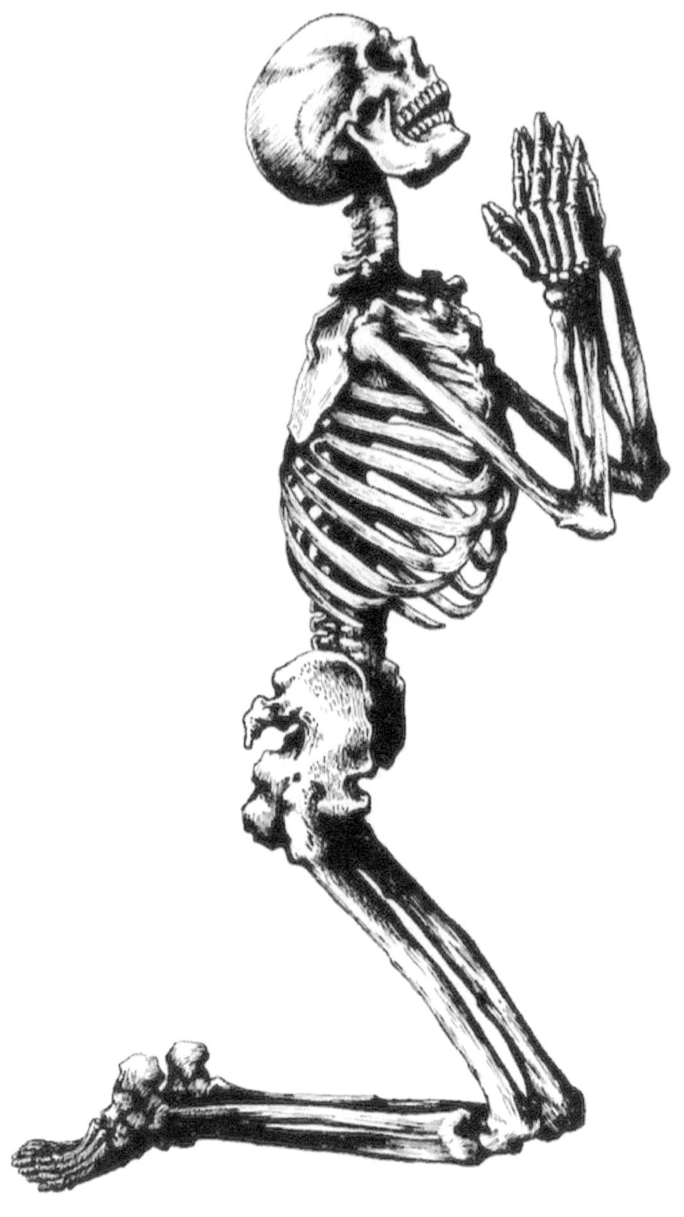

38. FAITH

I WISH I COULD MAGICALLY DISAPPEAR
TO THIS LAND,
WHERE I COULD LIVE WITH NO FEAR
WHERE PEOPLE ARE NOT CRUEL,
TO THE ONES WHO SEEM WEAKER.
WHERE EVERYONE BELIEVES THAT LOVE IS SOMETHING
THAT
BINDS US TOGETHER.
THAT YOU HAVE A CHOICE EVERYDAY,
TO LIVE WITH KINDNESS.
TO SPEARD PEACE IN A WORLD THAT IS AT CONSTANT
WAR WITH ITSELF.
I HOPE SOMEDAY,
WE ACHEIVE THIS GOAL
THAT I SINCERELY DREAM OF.
BUT I FEAR THAT,
FAITH IN HUMNITY IS LOST FOREVER.

39. STRONG

LONELINESS IS SOMETHING THAT EATS YOU ALIVE,
AND ESPECIALLY WHEN THIS HAPPENS JUST BECAUSE YOU
ARE BEING YOURSELF.
I WISH I KNEW THEN AND THERE,
THAT IT WASN'T MY FAULT.
I WISH SOMEONE HELD MY HAND, AND LED ME OUT OF
THE DARK
WHEN EVERYTHING WAS GOING WRONG,
JUST FOR HUMANITY'S SAKE.
ALL THESE YEARS OF MENTAL TORTURE,
JUST GONE
IF I KNEW HOW TO BE STRONG.

40. NEW

IT ALL SEEMS LIKE A FAIRYTALE
TOO GOOD TO BE TRUE,
BECAUSE NOTHING IS REAL IN THE WORLD OF FOOLS.
SINGING WITH THESE OLD STARS,
HOLDING ME WITH MY OWN ARMS
IT'S ALL NEW
CAN'T BELIEVE IT'S ALL TRUE
BECAUSE,
THIS WORLD HAS ALWAYS FELT SO BLUE.
STARTING FROM SCRATCH
A CLEAN SLATE,
BACK TO NEW

41. ~ ~ ~ ~ WHEN THE HEART STOPS BEATING

~ ~ ~ ~

THIS CHAPTER FOCUSES ON THE PEOPLE WHO WERE
NOTHING BUT BULLIES.
THIS CHAPTER IS ALL ABOUT HOW WORSE IT CAN GET
FOR A PERSON WHO IS CONSTANTLY BULLIED AND MADE
FUN OF.
THE ONES WHO ARE ALWAYS LEFT ALONE.
EVEN THE PEOPLE WHO YOU THOUGHT WERE YOUR
FRIENDS DITCH YOU JUST BECAUSE THEY DIDN'T WANT
TO BE ASSOCIATED WITH YOU.
WHEN YOU TRUST AND GIVE CHANCES AGAIN AND AGAIN,
SAYING IT WOULD BE THE LAST TIME YOU WOULD
THINKING THAT THINGS WOULD CHANGE THIS TIME
AROUND, BUT IT'S ALL THE SAME.
BLACK AND WHITE AS ALWAYS,
WHEN YOU JUST WANT THE COLOURS TO RETURN BACK.
YOU WANT TO FEEL SOMETHING OTHER THAN THIS -
HATE, AGONY, PAIN, SORROW.
JUST CONTENTMENT FOR ONCE.
AND AT ONE POINT YOU JUST GIVE UP,
WHEN EVERYTHING JUST GET'S TO MUCH,

*WHEN THE BEST OPTION YOU THINK IS NOTHING BUT TO
QUIT.*
ROSE PETALS,
IN DARK RED SHADE COLOUR
CAUGHT MY EYE
BUT THE ENDS WERE FULL OF SPIKES,
TOUCHED IT
MY FINGERS BLED,
TILL THERE WAS NOTHING LEFT IN ME.
THIS FRENZY,
THIS RUSH
FLED THROUGH MY VEINS
WHEN MY HEART STOPPED BEATING.

42. PARASITE

YEARS THAT PASSSED BY,
CAN'T BRING THEM BACK BY PRESSING REWIND
I UNDERSTAND WHY I TRUSTED THEM.
SNAKES SURROUND MY EYES,
BLINDING MY SIGHT.
THE SAYING ABOUT "HISTORY REPEATING ITSELF" IS TRUE
BECAUSE,
I HAVE BEEN HERE BEFORE
IT EVEN HURTS TODAY WHEN I THINK ABOUT IT,
I HAVE BEEN A PREY TO THESE PREDETORS BEFORE
THIS WILD HUNTS NEVER ENDS.
SO I STOPPED BELIEVING IN ANYONE ANYMORE,
EVERYBODY HERE LOOKS LIKE THEY ARE MADE OF GOLD
BUT THEY ARE ALL BUT A PARASITE.

43. GAME

I PAINT THIS PICTURE OF YOU EVERYDAY,
IT KILLS ME WITH EVERY PASSING SECOND AS I LOOK AT
IT
SLOWLY PRECISELY MENACINGLY;
IT'S A PERFECT PICTURE,
I BEING THE BEAUTY AND
YOU BEING THE BEAST.
A KILLER ASKING FOR REDEMPTION FROM ITS VICTIM.
IT WAS NEVER ABOUT FORGIVENESS,
JUST A CLEAN SLATE FOR YOU
TO START A NEW GAME.
BLEEDING IN FRONT OF YOUR EYES,
YOU WATCH, CALM AS EVER
I LAY ON THE GROUND,
YOU SHED A FEW TEARS OF JOY
ACTING AS IF I WAS NOTIIING
YOU MOVE ON TO ROLL THE DICE AGAIN.

44. WE NEVER LEARN

I AM ALWAYS STUCK IN THIS ENDLESS CYCLE OF
NOT BELIEVING THAT I AM ENOUGH.
I NEVER LEARN
I HAVE BEEN HERE BEFORE.

45. FOOL'S GOLD

SAW A PICTURE OF ME FROM A YEAR AGO
IT WAS A SHINNING DISTRACTION
WANTED TO BACK,
IT WAS ALL SO MELLOW.
I KNEW IT WOULD NEVER BE CONSTANT STAR,
I TURNED AROUND TO BE SOMEONE ELSE.
I ADMIT I AM WRONG,
BUT IT'S SOMETHING I WON'T FORGET.
I STILL FALL FOR THE ONES WHO SHOW ME THAT THEY
HAVE
SOMETHING IN THEM THAT I WOULD WANNA HOLD ON
TO.
FOR THEM I WOULD BLEED MYSELF DRY,
EVEN IF I KNOW WHAT THEY REALLY ARE.
I KNOW THEIR LOVE IS NOT REAL,
BUT I HOPE IT WAS.
I AM NOT DONE,
FALLING FOR THIS HOPE, THAT I SEEK IN YOU
FOOL'S GOLD.
SO SAVE ME OH LORD,
FOR THAT I CAN'T SAVE MYSELF
FROM THIS PERSON
THAT I WILL ALWAYS HAVE A SOFT SPOT FOR.
EVERY TIME I WANT TO LEAVE,

THEIR DECEPTIONS COME IN MY WAY
I KNOW THEY WILL LEAVE LIKE EVERYONE ONE DAY.
I LET THEM USE ME FROM THE VERY FIRST DAY,
I KNOW THEY ARE GOING TO HAVE A CHANGE OF HEART
WHEN I TELL THEM TO CHOOSE
BETWEEN ME AND
THE PEOPLE I WILL ALWAYS BE A NO-ONE TO.
BUT I AM STILL HERE WAITING FOR YOU,
FALLING AGAIN INTO THIS TRAP
FOOL'S GOLD.

46. PRETEND

CAN WE PRETEND JUST FOR A MOMENT,
AS THE CITY SLEEEPS
BECAUSE I KNOW WHEN THE SUN COMES UP,
I WON'T MATTER.
ALWAYS STUCK WHEN I THINK ABOUT WHAT I AM
FEELING,
DON'T WANNA BE AFRAID
OF THE PATH IT'S LEADING.
I KNOW THAT IT IS THE WAY TO HEALING,
I KNOW IT IS SOMETHING THAT I WILL LEARN WITH TIME.
EVERY THOUGHT OF YOU STARTS TO DOUBLE CROSS MY
MIND,
CRAWLING BACK TO THE DARK ROOM
CAUSE I DON'T WANNA FACE THE TRUTH,
THAT IS WAITING FOR ME IN THE LIGHT.
IT'S RAINING NOW,
NOBODY ASKED HOW I WAS,
TAKE MY DAYS,
TAKE AWAY ALL MY NIGHTS,
TAKE ME TO PARADISE.
PULL ME OUT,
I WANT TO BE SAFE.
IT WON'T LAST,
IT WILL COME AND PASS.

I FELT IT ALL,
I AM DONE NOW.
TAKE THIS AWAY,
CAN'T HELP BUT FELL EMPTY NOW.
I FEEL LOST, DON'T KNOW
WHICH DOOR TO KNOCK ON
WILL THEY EVEN ANSWER
I AM SUCH A LOST CAUSE.
I KNOW SOMEDAY THIS MASK WILL COME OFF,
SOMEONE WILL LOVE ME INSTEAD OF RUNNING OFF.
IT'S SAD HOW I SEEM TO FORGET EVERYTHING THEY DID,
AND TRY TO START NEW EVERYTIME.
I JUST DON'T WANT TO BE THE KID,
WHO IS ALWAYS CROSSED OFF
BUT THEY WANT SOMEONE
WHO THEY CAN PULL DOWN
JUST FOR A FEW FUN LAUGHS
HOW CAN PEOPLE DO THIS;
I DON'T WANNA FIGHT ANYMORE,
JUST TO END UP WHERE I WAS.

47. STOCKHOLM SYNDROME

YOU ARE HOLDING ME HOSTAGE,
I KNOW THERE WILL BE CONSEQUENCES.
SOMETHING'S TELLING ME TO STAY,
BELIEVE ME I KNOW IT'S NOT GONNA END WELL,
I KNOW I AM GOING TO BE HEARTBROKEN WHEN
EVERYTHING FALLS APART.
I MIGHT HAVE TO RUN,
IT CAN'T STAY THIS WAY
IT'S ALL SO BEAUTIFULLY WRONG.
BUT THERE'S NO OTHER PLACE,
I WOULD RATHER BE IN.

48. ILLUSIONS

LET'S GET OUT OF THIS TOWN,
AWAY FROM ALL THIS CHAOS.
AND I KNEW WHEN I SAID YES,
THIS IS GOING TO BE MY LAST.
HEAVEN CAN'T HELP ME NOW,
EVERYONE DOESN'T DESERVE TO BE SAVED.
BURNING EVERYTHING I SEE COMING MY WAY,
TRYING TO BE FREE, I BREATHED IN THE SMOKE.
WHEN THE SUN IS OUT,
I AM ON THE GROUND LAYING LOW
WAITING FOR THE MOMENT WHERE IT GETS TO ME,
I AM TIRED OF RUNNING FROM MY PAST.
AT LEAST IF I STOPPED RUNNING,
I CAN BE AT PEACE WITH MYSELF BY ACCEPTING MY FATE.
I AM STUCK IN MY OWN ILLUSIONS,
THE WORLD'S ENDING WON'T SUFFICE IT.
SO I LAY HERE LIFELESSLY,
WAITING FOR MY PAST TO TAKE FULL
CONTROL ON MY PRESENT.

49. FINAL SHOW

WELCOME TO THE FINAL SHOW
WIPE THE TEARS ON YOUR FACE,
YOU SHOULD BE RELIEVED THAT IT'S ENDING.
STOP CRYING;
YOU ARE GETTING AWAY FROM HERE FINALLY
IT WILL ALL BE ALRIGHT NOW,
THE END IS NEAR.
CLEAR THIS MIND OF YOURS,
FORGET ALL THE PAIN
THE BULLETS CAUSED.
I DON'T KNOW WHAT HAPPENS WHEN YOU LEAVE,
I JUST KNOW THE ONES WHO LOVE YOU
WILL ALWAYS REMEMBER YOU.
YOU HAVE A WHOLE ETERNITY
TO FORGET YOUR SORROW.
LET THE WINDS TAKE YOU AWAY,
SLOWLY TURNING TO ASH
AS THE WORLD AROUND YOU GOES SILENT.

50. ~ ~ ~ ~ GRATEFUL FOR YOU ~ ~ ~ ~

THIS CHAPTER IS ABOUT THE PEOPLE WHO HELD YOUR
HAND AND GAVE YOU STRENGTH
WHEN YOU NEEDED IT THE MOST
BEING THE PERSON WHO YOU COULD ALWAYS TURN TO
NO MATTER WHAT
ALWAYS BEING THE ONE WHO YOU COULD CALL
THEY WERE THE ONLY ONE WHO BELIEVED IN YOU
WHEN YOU DIDN'T EVEN BELIEVE IN YOURSELF
SUN COMES UP AFTER THE STORM
YOU WERE LIKE THE SHINNING RAY IN MY LIFE
THANK YOU FOR STAYING
I WILL ALWAYS BE GRATEFUL FOR YOU.

51. US

WE WERE BOTH WOUNDED
SAVED EACH OTHER FROM DROWNING
JUST A BREATH AWAY FROM GOING TO WASTE,
YOU TOOK IT ALL AWAY BY JUST BEING THERE.
WE IMAGINED THIS WORLD FOR US,
WHERE WE BOTH FELT LIKE WE WERE ENOUGH
SAFE FROM THE WORLD'S PRYING EYES.
THE SKIES WERE JUST MADE FOR US,
STARS WERE BRIGHTER WHEN YOU SMILED
HEART OF GOLD.
I KNOW YOU WOULD NEVER LET GO,
CAUSE YOU WERE ALWAYS THERE FOR ME
WHEN I NEEDED YOU THE MOST.

52. I AM SORRY

I AM NOT AFRAID OF LOVE,
I AM AFRAID OF PEOPLE TRYING TO FAKE IT
I HAVE HAD THAT MANY TIMES
I DON'T WANNA REPEAT MY WRONGS.
LEFT WHAT HURT ME ALL THAT TIME AGO,
I AM SORRY TO SAY THAT
I DON'T TRUST YOU
BUT I CARE SO MUCH
IS THAT SO WRONG.
WHEN I AM NOT WITH YOU I AM WEAKER,
SO HELP ME
BECAUSE I DON'T KNOW WHAT TO SAY
QUESTIONING MYSELF AS TO WHY
AM I ALWAYS SO TANGLED AND CONFUSED
DON'T WANNA WAIT TILL IT'S GONE.
WHAT SHOULD I DO WHEN,
I DON'T KNOW WHAT MY HEART WANTS
IS THAT SO WRONG.

53. A HELL LOOP

A PLACE THAT I CALL
MY HOME,
IS BURNING.
THE HINGES FROM THE DOOR BROKEN AND LEFT ON THE
FLOOR
THE EARTH BENEATH US SHATTERING TO THE CORE.
WE ARE NOT ONE FAMILY NOW,
JUST STRANGERS WHO ARE LIVING TOGETHER AS GHOSTS
OF EACH OTHER'S PASTS
SO EVIL
SO CRUEL
SO MISERABLE.
OUR HEARTS BLEED INFRONT OF OUR EYES,
WATCHING EACH OTHER AS WE SEEP INTO THE GROUND.
THE DEVIL ON OUR BACKS,
SMILING AS WE MURDER EACH OTHER WITH OUR OWN
HANDS
CARVING EACH OTHER'S HEART OUT WITH
THE DEVIL'S FORK
WHICH CRAVES FOR BLOOD AND PAIN
CALLING YOUR NAME
IT SEEKS OUT ALL THE BAD PARTS
THAT YOU LOATHE ABOUT YOURSELF
WHEN IT DOES FIND ITS WAY,

IT ANCHORS ITSELF WITH YOUR DEEPEST DARKEST SELF
AND STARTS TO BUILD ITSELF OVER YOUR DEAD GRAVE.
THE PAIN CAUSED BY YOUR OWN LOVED ONES,
THE MISERY THEY ENKINDLED
YOUR SOUL CRYING IN AGONY OF THE TURMOIL THEY
INFLICTED UPON YOU
HOW THEY SET EVERYTHING ON FIRE
LEFT YOU ON THE GROUND
AS THE FLAMES SWALLOW YOUR MEMORIES OF PURE
LOVE, PEACE AND JOY
THE MEMORIES YOU ONCE HELD WITH SO MUCH LOVE
AND PASSION
FEELINGS YOU CAN'T DESCRIBE IN WORDS
FEELINGS THAT CAN ONLY BE FELT
FEELINGS THAT EVERYONE SEEKS OUT FOR
LOOKING EVERYWHERE WITH NO LUCK
I ONCE SHARED THIS FEELING WITH SOMEONE.
KEPT UNDER DARKNESS FOR SO LONG,
THE LIGHT REACHED TO TAKE US TO OUR SAFE HAVENS
GIVING US AN ANOTHER CHANCE AT LOVE.
BUT WHAT HAPPENS WHEN EVERYTHING YOU THOUGHT
WAS TRUE,
JUST SUDDENLY WASHES OUT AND YOU SEE THE UGLY
TRUTH HIDING CHAOS BEHIND IT,
THE DECEPTION THAT IS LOVE
ALL OF IT
WAS JUST A BIG MASQUERADE
A FAKE NOTHINGNESS
YOUR WORLD CRUMBLES DOWN

WATCHING EVERYTHING FALL OUT AND DIE
SOMETHING YOU GREW WITH SO MUCH CARE AND LOVE
ALL HAPPY CHATTER NOW SEEMS LIKE MADNESS AND
BACKGROUND NOICE;
CHAOS
MAYHEM
A HELL LOOP AS I CALL IT.
EVERYTHING JUST DOESN'T MAKE SENSE TO ME
ANYMORE,
WHAT AM I SUPPOSED TO DO
AT THIS MOMENT
WHERE FAMILY IS MERELY BLOOD.
I LAY HERE TRYING TO BREAK FREE FROM THIS CAGE
BUT WHERE SHOULD I GO
WHEN I DON'T KNOW,
WHERE I BELONG.
CALLING STRANGES FOR HELP,
THEY WON'T UNDERSTAND WHERE I AM COMING FROM
THEY WILL LAUGH AT MY FACE
AND ACT LIKE
IT WAS ALL MY FAULT.
SO TAKE ME TO THE MOON,
WHERE THE LIGHT SHINES FOR ME IN THE DARKEST OF
NIGHTS.
I SPEND MY DAYS TRYING TO BREAK FREE,
FROM THE ONE'S THAT RULE MY HEART.

54. HOME

IS MY HEART IN THE RIGHT PLACE,
DO I KNOW WHERE I AM GOING?
BUT THE SUN WILL BE RISING
BACK HOME.
I FORGOT WHO I WAS FOR A MOMENT,
BUT I'll ALWAYS REMEMBER WHERE I BELONG.
ALL THIS TIME,
MADE SO MANY MEMORIES
THEY STAY IN MY HEAD LIKE A NIGHTMARE NOW.
LIGHTS FROM THE STARS SHINNING ON ME,
MAKING ME STRONGER THAN I EVER WAS.
I WAS NEVER REALLY ALONE,
ALWAYS WAITING FOR SOMEONE
TO TAKE ME HOME.
FOR YOU I FORGOT THE WAY TO REACH MY OWN,
ACCEPTED WRONGS WHEN THEY WERE YOURS.
FINALLY I MADE SOME CHANGES,
FROM THE HORIZON THE MOON WILL BE SHINNNG
BACK HOME.
ONE DAY THIS ALL WILL BE WORTH IT,
I WILL BE DREAMING OF HOPE AGAIN
I WON'T EVER FORGET WHERE I BELONG,
HOME.

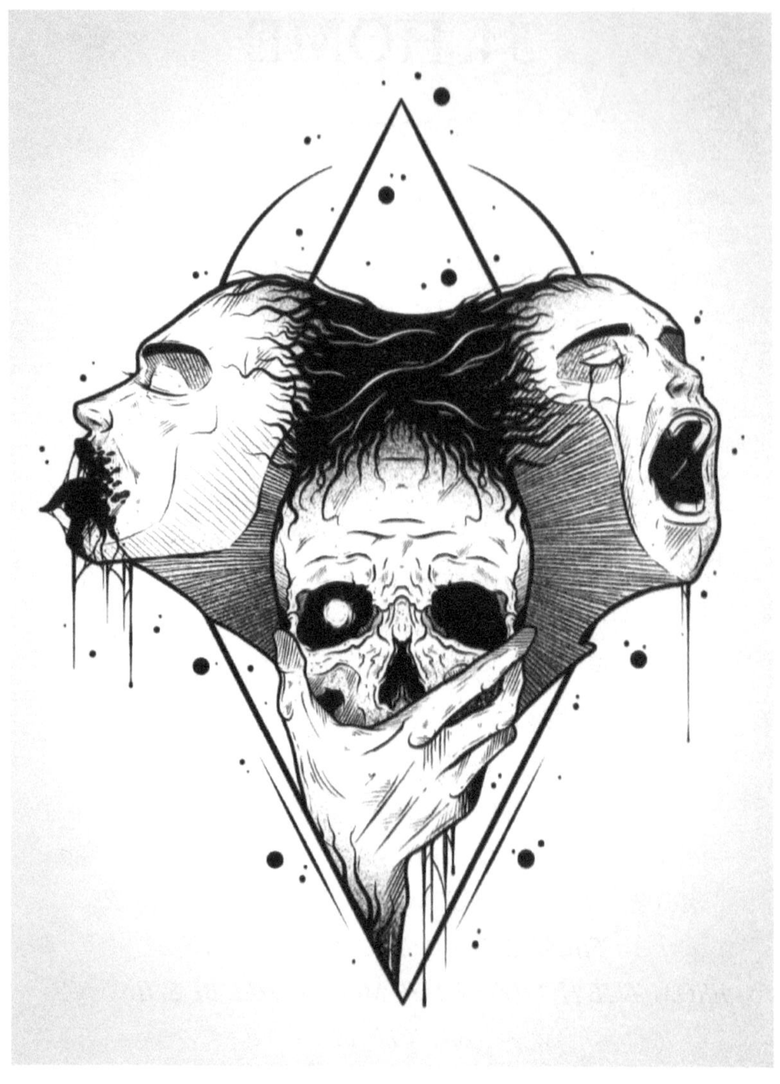

55. WHERE ARE YOU

I AM SEARCHING FOR A BROKEN HEART TO MAKE IT
WHOLE AGAIN,
WITH ITS OTHER HALF.
ALL THE WORDS YOU SPOKE,
GAVE ME STRENGTH TO FIND ONE FOR MY OWN.
ALL MY CRIMES,
LIVE IN MY CONCIOUS
FOREVER NOW.
I LEFT FOR A WALK,
SAW SOME SHADOWS
OF THE PEOPLE I LET DOWN,
EVERY PAWN THAT DIED MENDING MY HEART.
I AM AFRAID TO SAY SOMETHING BECAUSE I KNOW
IT WON'T MAKE A DIFFERENCE AT LAST
I DON'T THINK THEY WOULD EVER LOVE ME AGAIN.
I AM IN THE CORNER,
HOPING YOU WOULD SAVE ME AGAIN
A MY HIGHS
AT MY LOWS
YOU WERE ALWAYS THERE.
SO I SIT HERE TODAY
WAITING FOREVER FOR THE ONE
WHERE ARE YOU NOW.

56. YOU WILL ALWAYS FIND ME

DO YOU BELIEVE
IT'S ALL GONE?
BUT IF YOU LOOK,
YOU WOULD FIND ME IN THE REGION OF THE FADED
STARS.
NECESSARY FOR APOLOGIES BETWEEN US
NO,
THERE IS NONE.
I WILL ALWAYS REMEMBER YOU,
NO MATTER WHERE I GO
TO PLACES WE HAVE NEVER BEEN TO
ALWAYS FINDING EACH OTHER ON COMMON GROUND.
YESTERDAY I WENT TO SEE SOME FAMILIAR FACES,
THAT NOW CLAIM TO BE MY FRIENDS
I KNOW WHAT THEY SAY BEHIND MY BACK.
BUT YOU STAY THE ONLY ONE,
SAME AS YOU WERE
ALWAYS BY MY SIDE
NO MATTER WHAT HAPPENS.
THE FACT THAT WE CAN SIT TOGETHER RIGHT HERE AND,
SAY OUR GOODBYES
I JUST KNOW FOR A FACT

THAT WE'VE ALREADY WON.
NO,
IT'S NOT THE END
WE WILL SEE EACH OTHER AGAIN
OUT THERE
LIVING OUR BEST LIVING
BEING WHAT WE ALWAYS WANTED TO BE.
WE WILL BE RAISING A TOAST,
TO THE KIDS
WE LEFT BEHIND
WE WILL BE LAUGHING TO THE MEMORIES WE MADE
SOMETHING I WILL ALWAYS HOLD DEAR TO MY HEART.
YOU ARE LIKE THE COMPASS,
TO MY SHIP
KNOWING WHERE I'D BE.
YOU WILL ALWAYS FIND ME,
WALKING TOWARS YOU
TO REMEMBER,
TO MAKE,
MORE MEMORIES
OF THE LOVE THAT WE WILL ALWAYS SHARE.

57. ~ ~ ~ ~ I FINALLY MADE IT THROUGH ~ ~ ~ ~

ACCEPTANCE IS SOMETHING THAT IS VERY HARD TO
ACHIEVE.
NOT SAYING THAT I DON'T EVER FEEL DOWN ANYMORE,
I DO.
I STILL HAVE MY FAIR SHARE OF BAD DAYS, YOU WILL
ALWAYS HAVE THOSE.
BUT I CAN SAY THIS FOR SURE,
I AM CONTENT
FINALLY
I AM HAPPY.
THIS HAS BEEN A BEAUTIFUL JOURNEY THAT I EMBARKED
ON,
YES, THERE WERE SOME PARTS THAT I STILL FEAR TO EVEN
THINK UPON.
IN SIMPLE WORDS,
BY FAR THE MOST AGONIZING MOMENTS OF MY LIFE,
BUT I LEARNT SO MUCH, THESE TORTUROUS MOMENTS
PREPARED ME FOR THE WORLD.
THEY TAUGHT ME HOW TO BE STRONG FOR MYSELF.
I SAID MY LAST GOODBYE TO MY OLD SELF,
AND I WILL ALWAYS REMEMBER EVERYTHING.

IT IS SOMETHING TO REMEMBER I MUST SAY,
IT BROUGHT THE BEST IN ME.
I LEARNED LESSONS THAT ARE ALWAYS GOING TO HELP
ME BE THE BEST VERSION OF MYSELF.
SO HERE'S TO A NEW BEGINNING
TO A NEW ADVENTURE
TO A NEW CHAPTER
TO GROWING UP.
FINALLY I AM HERE
FINISHING THIS CHAPTER WITH TEARY EYES
MADE IT THROUGH
AND I WOULDN'T CHANGE A THING.

58. STEPPING INTO THE LIGHT

IN THE QUITE OF THE NIGHT,
I AM WAITING FOR AN ANGLE.
WINTER CHILLS IN THE MIDDLE OF A SUMMER NIGHT,
I SWITCHED OF THE LIGHTS
SAW SOMETHING SHINNING
IT WAS ALL VERY HAZY.
I SNUCK THROUGH THE GARDEN GATE,
IN SEARCH FOR ANSWERS.
THE CITY IS SLEEPING,
IT'S MIDNIGHT
AND SO I FOLLOWED THE LIGHT
BEEN WAITING SO LONG FOR THIS SIGHT.
WHEN I REACHED MY DESTINATION
I SAW A MIRROR,
I STOOD IN FRONT OF IT
I SAW AN ANGLE LOOKING BACK AT ME.
I STEPPED INTO THE LIGHT THAT DAY.

59. LOVING MYSELF WITH HALF A HEART

SIPPING TEA WITH BREAKFAST IN BED,
LIFE SEEMS EASY THESE DAYS
I THINK THIS BECAUSE,
LATELY IT'S BEEN HARD.
BUT I TRY,
LOVING MYSELF WITH HALF A HEART.
I LOOK PRETTY TODAY WITH A DRESS ON,
I SAY THIS BECAUSE
USUALLY IT IS SOMETHING I AM SCARED OF.
BUT I TRY,
LOVING MYSELF WITH HALF A HEART.
I DROVE PAST THE PEOPLE,
SAW THEIR FACES ALL LIT UP
STANDING ON THE GRAVE OF SOMEONE I KNEW,
THEY STILL SAY IT WAS ALL FAIR.
BUT I TRY,
LOVING MYSELF WITH HALF A HEART.

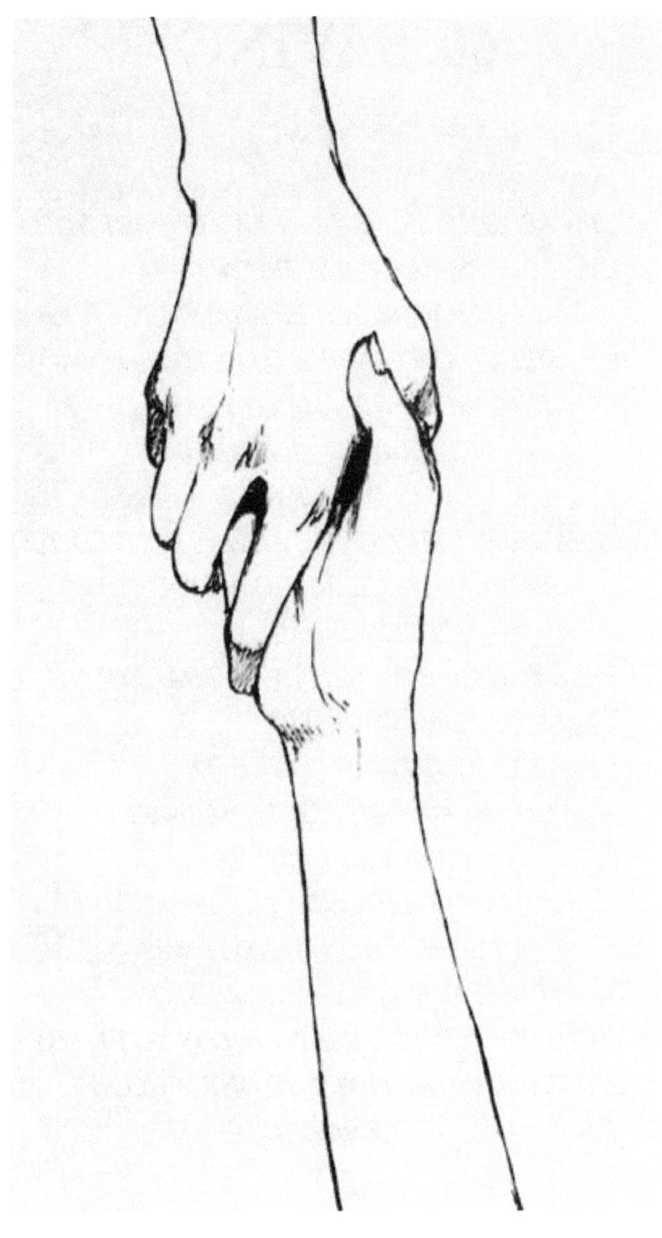

60. SAVING

TURN AROUND SEE WHAT'S WAITING FOR YOU
SPEAK YOUR TRUTH,
YOU WERE NEVER A SAINT.
SEE WHAT IT IS LIKE TO BE LOVED,
REACHING FOR A HAND TO HOLD
IT'S OKAY TO BE AFRAID.
CLOSE YOUR EYES,
AND DREAM SOMETHING YOU ALWAYS WANTED TO BE,
OPEN YOU EYES SEE WHO'S HAND IT IS
IT SEEMS SIMILAR,
LET IT TAKE YOU OUT OF THIS HOLE THAT YOU DUG FOR
YOURSELF.
SQUINTING YOUR EYES,
YOU SEE A BRIGHT LIGHT SHINNING
IT'S ALL SO LUCID.
AS YOU WALK TOWARDS THE END DOOR,
YOU SEE WHO'S HAND IT WAS
IT WAS YOU ALL THIS TIME ALONG.
NOW THE ONLY THING ON MY MIND IS TO BE THE ONE
WHO DID THE SAVING, NOT THE ONE WHO NEEDED TO
BE SAVED.

61. YOU

DEFENCESLESS AS I SHOW YOU MY HEART,
AND NOW I AM MORE VULNERABLE THAN I EVER WAS.
NOW I SHOW YOU MY SCARS,
TO LET THEM FINALLY HEAL FOR ONCE.
SO PAY ATTENTION WHEN I SAY THIS,
I NEED SOMEBODY TO LOVE ME
FOR WHO I AM AND ALWAYS WILL BE
HOPE THAT YOU DON'T RUN FROM ME.
I SWEAR,
TO ALWAYS REMEMBER THAT,
IT'S OKAY
TO SAY MY HEART OUT.
NOW I AM RIGHT BACK HOME TO YOU,
GAVE UP EVERYTHING TO LISTEN TO YOU
SO I AM STANDING TODAY HERE IN FRONT OF YOU
TO SAY THAT I WILL ALWAYS REMEMBER,
THAT YOU WOULD BE HERE NO MATTER WHAT.
I WOULD ALWAYS SAY THE TRUTH,
WHEN I CONFESS TO YOU
BECAUSE YOU KNOW MY HEART.
I AM HOME,
WHENEVER I PRAY TO YOU
I KNOW I WOULD NEVER BE ALONE,
WHEN THERE IS YOU

HOLDING MY HAND.
YOU BROUGHT BACK HOPE,
THAT I ONCE THOUGHT
WAS FOREVER LOST.

62. FINALLY CONTENT

THIS LAMP HAS A DULL WHITE LIGHT
WHEN I CLOSE MY EYES,
IT'S LIKE I AM CLOSE TO THE MOON ITSELF.
CLOSING MY LIDS,
THIS HAZY SPOT OF LIGHT STILL
REACHES MY SIGHT,
IT'S SO BEAUTIFUL.
I AM ON THE SWING,
ALONE IN CENTRAL PARK
LISTENING TO MY FAVOURITE TUNES,
IN THE DARK OF THE NIGHT.
I FEEL NOTHING OTHER THAN THIS SOLE SATISFACTION,
THIS FEELING OF ETERNAL CONTENTMENT
MY BRAIN FINALLY AT REST,
NO CHAOS AT LAST.
I FEEL THIS ENERGY RUSHING THROUGH ME,
THIS FEELING OF WARMTH IN THE COLDEST OF WINTERS.
I SMILED LIKE THIS AFTER SO LONG,
I WANT TO STAY LIKE THIS
FEELING BEAUTIFUL AT HEART.
THIS WORLD SURROUNDING ME IS SO SILENT,
EVERYBODY IS JUST WASHED OUT.
AS I FEEL THE BRISK WIND GUSTING AGAINST MY
SMOOTH SKIN,

I FEEL LIKE THE ONLY ONE LEFT
AND FOR THE FIRST TIME
IT'S THE BEST FEELING I HAVE EVER EXPERIENCED.

63. ALWAYS

REMEMBER WHEN YOU GAVE UP,
NOW I AM BLEEDING MY LOVE.
I DIED FOR YOU,
FOR THE LIGHT IN YOUR EYES TO RETAIN ITS GLINT
FOREVER
KEEEP THAT HOPE,
STAY AS YOU ARE.
NOW I SEE YOU,
AS I AM SEARCHING FOR A ROPE TO HOLD
PLEASE DON'T LET IT GO.
CATCH YOUR BREATH,
ALL WILL BE OKAY
YOU WILL FOREVER LIVE IN MY IMAGINATION.

64. I LOVE YOU

I KNEW A GIRL ONCE,
I WAS A CHILD BACK THEN
SHE HAD GORGROUS BROWN HAIR
EYES LIKE HONEY
MELTING DEARLY.
EYES THAT'll MAKE YOU CHOOSE LOVE EVERYDAY,
A FACE THAT WAS PURE INNOCENCE WHEN YOU LOOKED
AT IT,
SHE HAD THE COURAGE TO FIGHT THE WORLD ALL BY
HERSELF,
GOOD THAT COULD WASH OUT ANY EVIL THAT WAS EVER
CREATED,
A SMILE THAT COULD LIGHT UP THE DARKEST OF
WORLD'S,
KINDNESS THAT EVEN MADE THE HEARTLESS BELIEVE IN
LOVE.
BUT SOMEHOW SHE GOT LOST IN THIS CRUEL WORLD
SHE LIVED AROUND PEOPLE WHO DESPISED HER,
FOR WHO SHE WAS
SHE'D CRY EVERYDAY
UNTIL SHE WAS LEFT WITH NOTHING,
BUT EMPTINESS.
THE SPARKLE,
THE LIGHT

SHE HAD, FOREVER GONE.
THE HOLES IN HER BUTTERFLY WINGS,
SHE COULDN'T EVEN DREAM OF FLYING ANYMORE.
FACED ALL THE DARKNESS ALONE BY HERSELF,
SHE KNEW THAT SHE WAS TOO FAR GONE.
TIME FOR HER TO GAIN BACK EVERYTHING SHE ONCE
HAD WAS NEVER COMING BACK NOW,
IT WAS TOO LATE.
SHE COUDN'T BURDEN SOMEONE ELSE WITH HER
PROBLEMS,
PEOPLE AROUND HER WERE ALSO DEALING WITH THEIR
OWN STRUGGLES
SHE WOULD NEVER BLAME THEM FOR NOT NOTICING
HER MISERY,
SHE UNDERSTOOD THAT EVERYBODY WAS TOO CAUGHT
UP IN THEIR OWN CHAOS.
SHE BELIEVED IN SECOND CHANCES,
BUT IT ALL CAME CRASHING DOWN ON HER
WHEN THE MONSTERS SHE ONCE BELIEVED IN;
NOW CREEPED INTO HER HOUSE,
HAUNTING HER AT NIGHT
SHE HAD ALWAYS BEEN AFRAID OF THE DARK.
WHEN THE CLOUDS BECAME MERCY LESS STORMS,
THE RAIN FALLING FROM THE SKY
LOOKED LIKE TEARS SHE LET FALL,
IN TIMES OF COMPLETE HOPLESSNESS.
WINDOWS SHUTTERING LOUDLY,
THE NOICE WAS DRAINED OUT
WHEN SHE FOCUSED ON LISTENING TO HER HEARTBEAT

EVERY BEAT GAVE HER A NEW LIFE,
WHEN SHE JUST WANTED TO END IT ALL.
SHE WANTED UTTER SILENCE,
JUST EMPTINESS
THAT'S WHAT SHE WAS USED TOO
THAT'S THE ONLY THING SHE KNEW.
GOD I HOPE SOMEONE TOLD HER SHE WAS ENOUGH FOR
THE WORLD,
THAT SHE COULD STOP FIGHTING EVERYTHING AND
EVERYONE
SHE DESERVES ALL THE AFFECTION AND LOVE THERE IS
IN THE WORLD
THAT SHE MATTERED.
BUT WHEN SHE LOOKED AROUND,
THERE WAS NO ONE
DISSPOINTED BEACAUSE SHE THOUGHT SOMEONE
WOULD'VE ACTUALLY CARED.
I HOPE SHE FEELS PEACE NOW,
AT LAST
WHEN EVERYTHING IS GONE;
SHE CAN BE FREE NOW.
I LOOK UP IN THE SKY,
AND SEE HER WAVING BACK AT ME
WITH SO MUCH JOY AND LOVE.
I TELL HER HOW PROUD I AM THAT SHE WAS CREATED,
I AM HERE
AND I WILL ALWAYS LOVE YOU.

65. THOUGHTS OF MY SOUL ON A PAPER OF GOLD

THOUGHTS OF MY SOUL ON A PAPER OF GOLD,
SILENT PRAYES OF MY DREAMS
NEVER GO UNNOTICED IN HIS REALM OF PEACE
I LEARN THIS WITH EVERY PASSING MOMENT IN TIME
WITH THE MORNING SUN
AND WITH THE DROWNING NIGHT,
HE IS WITH ME THROUGH EVERY DARK PATH IN LIFE.
AS I SING THIS WITH ALL MY LOVE,
HARMONIES OF MY JOY
WILL REACH THE SKY AND ABOVE.

Author's Note

SO I STARTED TO WRITE THIS BOOK LAST YEAR,

IN 2021.

I HAD ALL THESE THOUGHTS THAT I WANTED TO WRITE DOWN AND

BASICALLY SHARE SOME OF MY EXPERIENCES.

THIS BOOK DEALS WITH ~

COMMON ISSUES THAT TEENAGERS DEAL WITH ON A DAILY BASES.

EVERYBODY EXPERIENCES BULLYING AND SOME TYPE OF MENTAL ABUSE AT SOME POINT IN THEIR LIFE.

I HAVE DEALT WITH BULLYING FOR THE PAST 11 YEARS

AND I AM 14 YEARS OLD AS OF NOW.

PEOPLE DID THEIR BEST TO ALWAYS MAKE ME THE OUTCAST,

SOME TIMES THEY WERE MY PEERS

SOME TIMES THEY WERE MY CLOSE RELATIVES.

THEY ALL MADE ME FEEL LIKE EVERYTHING BAD THAT WAS HAPPENING AROUND ME WAS MY FAULT.

AT THE YOUNG AGE OF 10 I WAS LOST AND AFRAID TO BE IN A ROOM

FULL OF PEOPLE.

I FELT LIKE EVERYBODY WAS WATCHING ME AND CONSTANTLY JUDGING.

ALWAYS OVERTHING ABOUT HOW I LOOKED LIKE

OBSESSING OVER EVERY LITTLE THING.

I JUST DIDN'T WANT TO BE MADE FUN OF,

NOBODY WANTS THAT.

I WAS EMBARRASSED OF MY OWN SELF.

I WANTED TO BE SOMEONE WHO WAS GOOD ENOUGH FOR THE WORLD,

IN DOING THAT I LOST MYSELF AS A PERSON.

I HAD ALWAYS BEEN THE KID WHO SAT ALONE IN EVERY CLASS,

THE KID WHO NOBODY EVER SPOKE TO.

I REMEMBER HOW EVERYONE WAS ALWAYS SO EXCITED TO MEET THEIR FRIENDS AT SCHOOL

BUT WHEN I LOOKED AT MYSELF,

I WAS ALWAYS FINDING EXCUSES TO NOT GO TO SCHOOL

I WAS SCARED TO FACE EVERYONE THERE.

IT WAS LIKE I WAS STUCK WITH PEOPLE WHO TREATED ME LIKE I WAS NOTHING.

I WAS CONSTANTLY LEFT ALONE IN EVERYTHING.

AND THE TEACHERS WERE NO BETTER,

IF I AM BEING HONEST.

WHENEVER SOMEONE DID TALK TO ME EVEN THE SLIGHTEST BIT,

I REMEMBER HOW EXCITED AND HAPPY I WOULD GET TO TELL MY MOM ALL ABOUT THE NEW FRIEND I MADE AT

SCHOOL.

BUT WHENEVER I THOUGHT THAT I WAS FINALLY GETTING SOMWHERE

WHENEVER I THOUGHT THAT THIS MISERY OF ALWAYS FEELING ALONE WOULD GO AWAY,

I WOULD JUST END UP WHERE I WAS BEFORE.

NOTHING WOULD EVER CHANGE,

IT WAS ALWAYS THE SAME.

THEN ONE DAY EVERYONE JUST STARTED TO FADE AWAY,

AS I CREATED THESE WALLS AROUND ME

I PROMISED MYSELF THAT I WOULDN'T LET ANYBODY IN

I WAS TOO HURT TO EVEN TRY

AND WHY WOULDN'T I BE HURT

EVERY ONE THAT I TRUSTED EVEN THE ONES WHO STAYED AROUND FOR A BIT,

LEFT AT THE END.

I KNEW THEN AND THERE THAT

NOBODY ACTUALLY STAYS FOREVER

YOU ARE ALWAYS ALONE AT THE END.

IN THIS WORLD,

YOU ARE THE ONLY ONE WHO IS THERE FOR YOURSELF.

THIS IS A JOURNEY I WENT THROUGH,

THE COUNTLESS NIGHTS WHERE I'D CRY MYSELF TO SLEEP.

I REMEMBER ALL THE NIGHTS THAT I REMINDED MYSELF,

THAT IT WAS ALL GOING TO BE OKAY,

THAT I SURVIVED YET ANOTHER DAY,

THAT ONCE I AM OLDER I WOULD KNOW WHAT TO DO.

I STILL TELL MYSELF THESE THINGS.

DON'T GET ME WRONG

I ALWAYS HAD MY FAMILY AND I DID TALK TO THEM ABOUT THESE THINGS

AND EVERYONE DID THE BEST THEY COULD DO TO HELP.

MY FAMILY WAS ALWAYS THERE FOR ME.

I NEVER DOUBTED THAT.

IT WAS JUST THAT I MYSELF DIDN'T KNOW HOW MUCH IT AFFECTED ME.

BECAUSE I NEVER WANTED TO OPEN THIS DOOR THAT LED TO THESE MEMORIES OF MY PAST THAT I JUST DIDN'T WANT TO DEAL WITH AT ALL.

I LIVED A DOUBLE LIFE,

I WAS A HAPPY, CHEERY GIRL

WHO EVERYBODY LOOKED AT AND THOUGHT THAT SHE WAS FINE.

BUT WHEN I WAS ALL ALONE,

I FELT ALL THESE BUILT UP EMOTIONS ON AN ANOTHER LEVEL OF INTENSITY,

EVERYTHING JUST HIT ME AT ONCE

THEN I WOULD BREAKDOWN AND

LOCK AWAY EVERYTHING AT ONE CORNER AND NEVER LOOK IN ITS DIRECTION EVER AGAIN.

THAT'S HOW I DEALT WITH THINGS

I WAS AN ESCAPE ARTIST.

WHAT I DIDN'T KNOW WAS THAT NOT DEALING WITH EMOTIONS LIKE THESE

WOULD AFFECT ME IN THE FUTURE SO MUCH,

AND THAT'S EXACTLY WHAT HAPPENED.

MY PAST FINALLY CAUGHT UP TO MY PRESENT,

AND MADE IT MORE MISERABLE THAN EVER.

THE PROBLEM WAS,

THAT I DIDN'T KNOW WHAT WAS THE CAUSE TO THIS CATASTROPHE.

THIS PIT THAT I ALWAYS FELT,

THIS DEPRESSING FEELING.

WHY WAS I SUDDENLY FEELING SO OVERWHELMED BY EVERYTHING THAT WAS GOING ON AROUND ME?

SO IN ORDER TO ACTUALLY KNOW WHAT I WAS FEELING,

I STARTED TO WRITE WHATEVER CAME TO MIND.

THEN IT ALL JUST STARTED TO LINE UP,

I UNDERSTOOD MYSELF BETTER.

I REVISITED MEMORIES THAT I WANTED LOCKED AWAY FOREVER,

I DEALT WITH THE MONSTERS THAT HAUNTED ME EVERY NIGHT.

I LEARNT SO MUCH ABOUT MYSELF BY DOING THIS

BECAUSE THERE IS NO ONE WHO KNOWS YOU BETTER THAN YOURSELF.

WHEN I WROTE THIS BOOK,

I WAS PURELY FOCUSING ON THE SOLE PURPOSE OF TELLING MY STORY.

EVERY GOOD OR BAD THING THAT I HAVE BEEN THROUGH,

EVERY THING THAT MADE AN IMPACT ON MY LIFE,

FROM EVERYTHING I LOVE TO EVERYTHING I HATE

FROM EVERYTHING I REGRET TO EVERYTHING I AM PROUD OF

THIS IS ME

WITHOUT ANY HIDDEN MASKS

POURING MY HEART OUT

FINALLY LETTING THE WORLD KNOW THAT

I AM READY TO START A NEW CHAPTER NOW.

THANKYOU FOR READING

IT REALLY MEANS ALOT

HOPE YOU LIKED IT

- SEHAJ KAUR.

www.ingramcontent.com/pod-product-compliance
Lightning Source LLC
Chambersburg PA
CBHW031409150726
47989CB00002B/587